ISHI
The Last of His People

By David Petersen

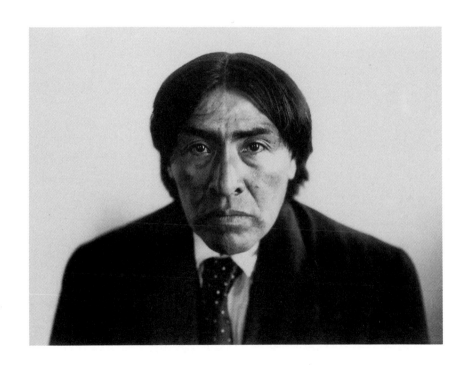

CHILDRENS PRESS ®

CHICAGO

PHOTO CREDITS

California State Library — Cover (neg. #19,564), 8 (neg. #19,389), 9, 18 (neg. #172a), 26 (neg. #19,565)

Lowie Museum of Anthropology, The University of California at Berkeley — 3, 6, 10, 11, 12, 15, 16, 17, 22, 24, 25, 27, 29, 30, 31

Maps by Donald Charles — 14, 19

Project Editor: E. Russell Primm III
Design and Electronic Composition: Biner Design
Photo Research: Judy Feldman

Library of Congress Cataloging-in-Publication Data

Petersen, David
    Ishi : the last of his people / by David Petersen.
    p. cm. — (Picture-story biography)
    Summary: Recounts the life of Ishi, sole survivor of a small band of Yahi Indians, who was found in 1911 near Oroville, California.
    ISBN 0-516-04179-7
    1. Ishi, d. 1916 — Juvenile literature. 2. Yana Indians — Biography — Juvenile literature. [1. Ishi, d. 1916. 2. Yana Indians — Biography. 3. Indians of North America — California — Biography.] I. Title. II. Series: Picture-story biographies.

E99.Y23I846 1991   90-28887
979.4'004975   CIP
[B]   AC
[92]

ISHI

The Last of His People

It all began on the morning of August 29, 1911, near the little town of Oroville, in northern California.

Just after daylight, dogs began barking outside the town's slaughterhouse. When the workers went outside, they could hardly believe what they saw. The dogs had forced an Indian man into the corner of the

corral, where he had probably come for food. And what a strange looking fellow he was!

The man, of medium height, looked about fifty years old. He was naked except for a piece of canvas worn around his shoulders like a poncho. His skin was coppery brown. His hair was cropped short. His nose and both his ears were pierced, and from his earlobes hung pieces of deer hide. He was so thin that the men could easily have counted his ribs.

Although they couldn't have known it, the workers were looking at what may have been the last Indian in North America living in the wild. Other Native Americans had long ago become part of American society.

Ishi as he looked soon after he wandered into
Oroville, California, August 29, 1911.

Even the famous Apache warrior Geronimo had surrendered some twenty-five years earlier.

The workers called off the dogs and sent for the sheriff. When Sheriff J.B. Webber arrived, he led the frightened man peacefully away to the Oroville jail. Webber was a kind, decent man

Ishi soon became a popular subject for photographers both in San Francisco and Oroville.

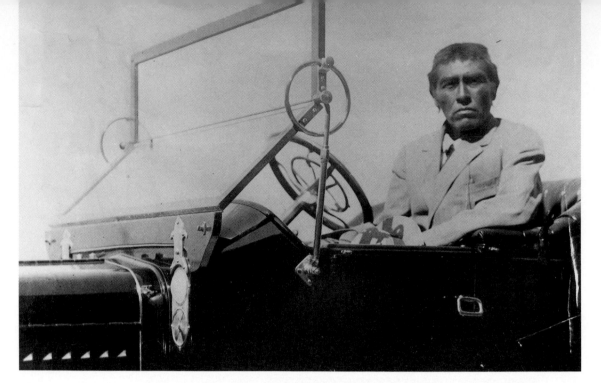

Ishi in a car soon after his appearance in Oroville.

and had decided to put the stranger in jail not as a criminal, but to give him a safe place to rest and recover.

The sheriff now had a problem. What was he to do with this poor fellow who could speak no English? He gladly gave him food and clothing. But he couldn't keep him in jail forever. The man had not committed any crime.

As the story of the man quickly spread through the California newspapers, a solution presented itself. Within a couple of weeks, Webber received a telegram from a professor of anthropology (the study of human cultures) at the University of California in San Francisco. The professor had read about the mysterious Indian and said he'd like to

bring him to the university. There, one of the anthropologists might know his language and be able to talk with him.

Eager to pass along responsibility for the Indian, Sheriff Webber agreed.

The man who came to communicate with the Indian was also a professor at the university. His name was Thomas Waterman. He quickly won the Indian's trust by speaking a few words

Professor
T. T. Waterman.

in his native language. Waterman guessed correctly that the Indian was a member of the Yahi tribe, southernmost of the four tribes of the Yana nation. This tribe had been thought to be extinct. Because it was considered rude in Yana culture for a man to speak his given name, eventually the Americans would call the stranger "Ishi," the Yana word for "man."

Once, the Yana nation had numbered in the thousands, and the Yahi tribe in the hundreds. Their homeland had been the steep, rocky country south and west of the extinct volcano called Mount Lassen, in northern California. For thousands of years, the Northern, Central, Southern, and Yahi tribes of the Yana nation had lived proudly. They lived in balance with nature.

The Yana nation was located in north central California.

They did no farming. They kept no livestock. The Yana had no metals and no wheels. Their weapons and tools were simple and made from wood, bone, and stone.

Yana men used bows and arrows to hunt deer and set traps for rabbits. To catch the salmon that swam in the clear, fast-flowing streams, they made

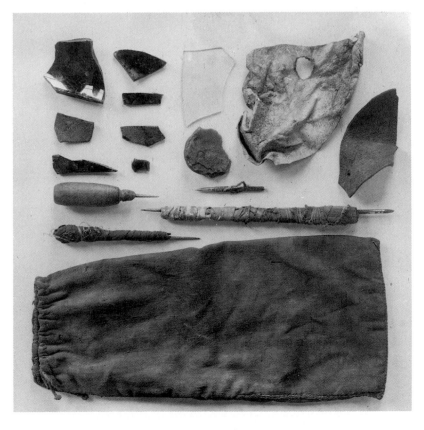

A Yana arrow-making outfit of the type Ishi would have used (top); Ishi's arrow-making kit (bottom).

Ishi demonstrated for his new friends the proper use of a bow and arrow.

wicker fish traps, handwoven nets, and wooden spears.

Yana women and children gathered green spring clover, roots, and other wild plants that they could eat. Their most important food, however, was the acorn, or oak nut. After soaking and rinsing the acorns in water to get rid of their bitter taste, the nuts were stone-ground into flour. The flour was then packed into woven baskets for storage. In winter, a Yana wife would mix water with some of the acorn flour. She then boiled it to make a hot cereal for her family.

The Yana lived in small, simple houses made of tree limbs, bark, and

Ishi and the house he built on the grounds of the museum.

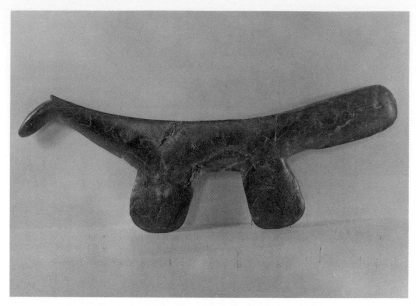

An example of Indian stone carving.

brush. In summer, when the weather was warm, they went almost naked. In winter, they wore warm cloaks of rabbit skins and feathers. Their needs were few.

But the days of this life would soon end. Gold was discovered along the creeks and rivers of northern California in 1849. Miners and settlers soon began arriving from the East. They came by the thousands. Some

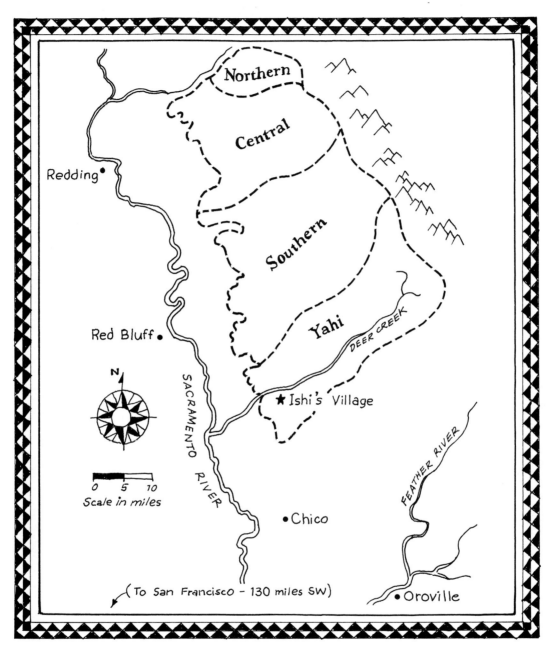

Map of the Yana territory.

settled in Yana country, built houses, and took up farming or ranching.

This created a dangerous situation. To the Yana, the settlers were invaders. The Americans stole their land and treated them badly. The whites, or *saldu* in the Yana language, also scared away or killed the wild animals. This robbed the Yana of an important source of food. For this reason, when they got very hungry, desperate Yana sometimes broke into settlers' homes looking for food. They also sometimes stole sheep and cattle to feed their families.

The settlers soon viewed the Yana as thieves. Looking for revenge, some angry settlers formed groups, called vigilantes, to chase down and kill the "thieves."

For twenty-five years the fighting between settlers and Yana continued. The *saldu* had guns and horses, while the Indians had only bows, arrows, and their bare feet. Only a handful of settlers were killed by Indians. Thousands of Yana men, women, and children, almost all of them innocent of any wrongdoing, were killed by the settlers.

Sometime between 1860 and 1862, in the middle of all the fighting and killing, Ishi was born.

By the late 1800s, fewer than twenty of the Yana people survived. Of Ishi's tribe, the Yahi, only five remained. To keep from being hunted down and killed, Ishi, his mother, and his sister were forced to live in hiding. This was a hard life. After a while only one Yahi was left: Ishi. Ishi lived alone in hiding for several years before he wandered into Oroville.

When Ishi arrived in Oroville, he was mourning for his dead mother and sister. In fact, he was prepared to die. He expected to be shot on sight or hanged.

The days of the California vigilantes were over. Through the kindness of Sheriff Webber and the professors from the university, Ishi suddenly had new hope.

What a strange and frightening experience the long train ride from Oroville to San Francisco must have been for Ishi. All his life, he had spied on this strange creature. It ran on tracks, breathed out smoke, spoke with a scream, and carried people in its belly. His mother had called it the *saldu* monster. Now, he was riding in the monster's belly!

Affiliated Colleges as they appeared in 1912: Dentistry and Pharmacy (left), Hospital (center), and Museum (right).

When the train arrived at San Francisco, Professor Waterman took Ishi to the university. A comfortable room in the school's Museum of Anthropology building would be his new home. The museum's director was Professor A. L. Kroeber. He was the man who had sent the telegram to Sheriff Webber. It was Kroeber who gave Ishi his name.

Already, Ishi had two friends. Later, there would be a third — Saxton Pope, a doctor from the university's medical school. Dr. Pope, like Ishi, loved to shoot with a bow and arrows. They spent many hours together practicing.

Saxton Pope, M.D.

Ishi eventually learned several hundred words of English, saying them with a strong Yana accent. Ishi soon lost his shyness and became a celebrity in San Francisco. Almost every Sunday, crowds of people would come to watch him demonstrate his people's crafts. From a tree limb, he would fashion a graceful hunting bow. From

Sam Batwi, A. L. Kroeber, and Ishi, 1911.

In September 1911, Ishi attended a show at the Orpheum Theatre. The star of the show, Lily Lena, is seated to the left behind Ishi.

a piece of black rock, called obsidian, he would chip sharp arrowheads. He could even make fire by rubbing sticks together. The people of San Francisco loved Ishi.

In May 1914, after three years at the museum, Ishi and his three friends decided to travel to Ishi's homeland in the foothills of Mount Lassen. There, they camped near where Ishi had lived.

Back in San Francisco, Ishi's friends had helped him learn to live in his new world. Now it was Ishi's turn to be the teacher. With bows and arrows, he taught Dr. Pope to hunt deer and other animals. Using a forked stick, Ishi showed Professor Kroeber how to balance on a rock in a rushing stream and spear salmon. He and Waterman collected and identified native plants that Ishi's people had eaten and used as medicines.

Together, the four men climbed the rocky cliffs, explored the caves, and swam in the clear, cold creeks. Their

Professor Kroeber photographed during his month-long trip with
Ishi to the Yana homeland.

month-long vacation in the Yahi homeland passed very quickly.

Soon after returning to San Francisco, Ishi fell ill with a serious lung illness called tuberculosis. In the wild, Ishi had never been sick. Therefore, he had not developed an immunity to many diseases. Now he was dying from one of the worst of them. Nonetheless, he remained brave and cheerful to the end. After four years and seven months at the anthropology museum, Ishi died on March 25, 1916. No one ever learned his true name. Still, he would not be forgotten.

To the world that Ishi had stumbled into, he would remain forever the last reminder of a primitive time. To those who knew him, he would be remembered as a gentle, intelligent, and loyal friend.

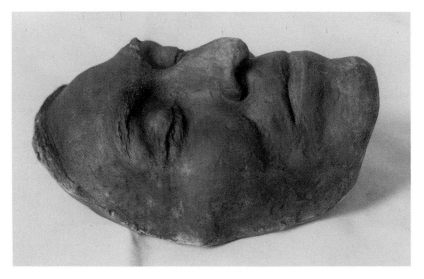

Ishi's death mask.

ISHI

c. 2,000 – 1,000 B.C.	Ancestral Yana Indians first occupy northern California
1850	Gold seekers invade Yana homelands, following the Old Lassen Trail. Destruction of Yana by white settlers begins, the goal being total extermination.
1860–1862	Ishi is born.
1908	November 9—A survey party stumbles upon the small, carefully hidden village of the last five surviving Yahi. The inhabitants scatter in panic; Ishi's mother dies soon after, and he never sees his sister again.
1911	August 29—Ishi wanders into Oroville, California.
	September 4—Ishi leaves with Professor Waterman to live at the University of California at San Francisco.
1915	May—Ishi, Kroeber, Waterman, and Pope return to the Yahi homeland for a month-long camping and research trip.
1916	March 25—Ishi dies of tuberculosis in San Francisco.

INDEX

ACKNOWLEDGMENT

The author wishes to acknowledge Theodora Kroeber, wife of the late Dr. Alfred Kroeber and author of *Ishi in Two Worlds*. Mrs. Kroeber's book is the preeminent biography of Ishi and, as such, has served as the primary source for facts in this book.

ABOUT THE AUTHOR

David Petersen lives with his wife and dog in a cabin high in the mountains of southwestern Colorado. He is the author of *Among the Elk* and other adult books. This is his ninth book for Childrens Press.